COMET WINE

RUTH TAYLOR
COMET WINE

Edited by Endre Farkas
Book design by Terry Gallagher/Doowah Design Inc.
Author photo by Abe Sosnowicz
Printed and bound in Canada

The following poems appeared in the chapbook *A Taste of Comet Wine*, 1999: "A Poet's Work," "Sweet, Raw Love Never Mocks," "Disembodiment," "Here Stops the Mystery of Hermes and Hekate," and "To the Poets of the World."

We acknowledge the financial support of the Manitoba Arts Council, The Canada Council for the Arts and the Government of Canada through the Book Publishing Industry Development Program (BPIDP) for our publishing program.

Library and Archives Canada Cataloguing in Publication

Taylor, Ruth, 1961-2006.
Comet wine/Ruth Taylor.

Poems.
ISBN 978-1-897289-17-4

I. Title.
PS8589.A96C66 2007 C811'.54 C2007-901332-5

J. Gordon Shillingford Publishing
P.O. Box 86, RPO Corydon Avenue, Winnipeg, MB Canada R3M 3S3

*The editor would like to thank Odette Dubé
for her fine proofreading.*

Table of Contents

Foreword

Comet Wine is Ruth Taylor's third and final book. Unfortunately, she died before she could see it published. Fortunately, however, she had finished 99.9 percent of it. The last time we talked about *Comet Wine*, she said it was one poem away from completion. I believe that with "Envoi", she did complete the manuscript.

Ruth had already determined the order of the poems and it is her sequencing that is presented here. I have made only three editorial incursions: I've capitalized the first letter of each word of each first line, whether it was a new sentence or not, included her "Comet Wine (notes toward a consolidation)" as the introduction, and I have added one poem "The Marriage of Heaven and Earth" at the end.

I decided on the capitalization because her manuscript was inconsistent. While some of her choices made sense, others did not; they appeared to be the result of computer default decisions rather than her conscious ones. I decided to go with this kind of capitalization because, aside from being a convention which she had used before, it also gives the poems structural harmony.

Her "notes toward a consolidation," which was buried in an earlier version, seemed to be the ideal introduction. It is a private meditation on the book and a public musing that was heading towards being an introduction. And as for the inclusion of "The Marriage of Heaven and Earth," I did this because it is a fine poem and she had written it during this period.

Endre Farkas

Comet Wine (notes toward a consolidation)

If any book is opened there will be revealed messages of such import as might shock the open circuits into greater reach. Among dancers, the space between them dances as well, among entities engaged in similar work [there is] a deep connection. It is this connectedness and the search for it which have powered this exploration, the secret journey that is undertaken when the World and its Laws loom too large for the psyche in pursuit of oneness. For the World's Laws are ever written to confound and thereby prevent any pilgrimage into Love's Mysteries, for it is not in the interests of the World that any don the yoke of freedom. And the battle has been raging since first we entered flesh, and hence, what was at inception intended to conjoin heaven and earth in mystical marriage, thus completing the hat trick alchemical process (not only self and other but self, self and other as the doubled un-self—but this will need a careful explanation as the metaphors emerge) whence, in the Tarots, The Lovers, The Devil, The World, The Chariot, the Three of any Suit. The point of the mystic marriage, in the first place, was creation—the generation of consciousness that can out of its own will invent and manifest the entirely new and unprecedented. All entities at this moment in the flesh are involved in the gowning of the bride, all are hearing the loud, unexplained silence that anticipates Heaven and the Triumph of Yes and Yes. But here's the rub: the flesh does not wish to marry and has claimed hold of the indwelling energy, and holds it ransom. It wishes to be paid in immortality, has never understood itself the vehicle, has been taught by the World that the potter ranks no higher than the clay.

Ruth Taylor

Prelude (A Poet's Work)

What is the poet's Work?
And why and oh why and oh why
To be in the world and sometimes of it
To be of the world and sometimes in it
To be out of it and sometimes with it
To spit out bitmapped stars, earth, sky
To deceive and to wax bucolic
With Magus, Mystic, Alcoholic,
In a labyrinth, with dread absinthe
And keep callow sanity at bay

To bay at new vintage moons
In sultry dew smooched gloam
And for the sake of it
Lounge dishabilled a-shamble
In briar and bramble
And on cool deep woods loam

To be spaced-out
In inner/outer space
Indifferent and laconic, gung-ho, sardonic,
Verbose, catatonic, meek, supersonic,
Grim, austere and euphonic,
Biological, prophetic, incoherent, moronic…
To offer a hot sweet sour and bitter tonic

To love the wrong person
Indefinitely

To have too much occasionally
And too little most of the time

To record the pique and rasp
Of random rain
The goad of slick glissando
The miscellany of loose desires
The reproach of harvest coloured hair

The twist in a Liar's stare
The Lie in the Exorcist's prayer
The relief of a yawn's ritardando

To blow people away
And to blow them off
To skate a lemniscate before hostile judges
Between extremes of knowing

To love the wrong person
Integrally
And to wait too long

To never wait long enough
For rogues and rakes and wraiths and wretches
For freaks and fakes and fiends and fetches
To write down phone numbers
And lose them

To have one too many,
One too few
To compose eloquent curses
To distribute blessings and boons
To memorize lines from Looney Tunes
To dream canned gods and goddesses
And give a damn

To be the victim of a headmail spam
To travel with a backpack full of rocks
To extract a coyote's tooth
To grow thistles

To dance naked in sheet lightning
And crank up the heat
To be frightening
And love the wrong person
Meteorically

To sometimes be of it
To run red lights occasionally,

To trip while carrying something delicate
And to watch hockey distractedly
Not caring if anyone scores

To cruise the moon in moonless topless bars
To tap out bawdy tunes
On the hoods of police cars
To be apart from it
And a party to it all

To croon somber solos
To moan out laughter
To love the wrong person
Impertinently

To love loving the wrong person
Paradoxically, pathologically
To roll an oak wheel
Down a blind Babylonian alley
To jump through silver hoops
Held up by flatulent Shriners

To not always love
The same wrong person
Exclusively

To love a different wrong person
As often as is necessary
To leave and arrive on cue

To dally among the stars
Hang out in bars
And love everyone
Eventually

To be in the stars
And of them

To write poems
That are misunderstood.

Prologue

Herewith unfurls a tale in rhymes mysterious
Of Love's sweet tricks and of Love's sorrows
As visited upon machines mortal and fickle
Layered upon dry splinters of bones, rare clays
Of rare earth and sublime heavenly infusions.
Oh I sing Love's blundering baroque confusions
Burlesque torment even to the remote Gods
Of oxygen-rich antediluvian days
Love's Plow, Love's Yield, Love's Harvest Sickle,
Love's Dreams, Delusions and Ardent Arrows
And Love's Fevers full of visions delirious.
And all to the marriage of Earth and Heaven
For nought transforms without Love's Leaven.

Intimate Limits

I

No insipid marginal gloss, no melancholic pencilling
Does justice to this illness—no miasmic stalkers
From the dark matter swamp will be mistaken for alien visitors—I
Am less than hallucination, a mere exobiological toy
From star-cluster-headache space, ga-ga-lactic
Self masquerades as quasar static, quantum joy

I come to (I: a two-bit crook)
And speak—for what!

No phoenix will fly by
And drop hot solar strawberries
Into my mouth, I'll hit no jackpot
Of ill-gotten quarters
In the phone booth   even a friend's
Home-grown cayennes are not
Bright incisors
Erotic tongues
Fervid Pentecostal Flares, thus
All is but a disbursement
Of Day-Glo magma
Another speech
Another febrific fuss
Or else
The silences in this making
Are in this making
Silences

II

Yet, there is need for poles and fixed stars
There is need for earthquake lights
And between "need" and "lights" unseen
A patterning of pattern's disappearance
And between disappearances, art without object
Its longness fugitive

'Tis dry, 'tis dry, 'tis parched
Fibers in a parchment, filaments in damask,
Features printed in a shroud
A tract in stigmata or Linear B.

There are small owls
And through rotchinks in old barnwood
One may chance a glance
Gibbous of moon in one wild nocturnal eye
Or steal, a furtive field mouse
Across a beam—but who

Who in cities clandestine of rendezvous
And late in this age of maximum torque
Is but a tasty morsel on a gleaming plate
You

You: a shiver between blinks
Life and Death in a sidelong squint.

III

Lifeline, heart line, headline, line of fate.
Our palms tell us nothing, nor do the oracles we cast
In rare private moments explain
How we are quivering palsies of nerves
Grotesquely wasting oxygen

Would that we could taste
The powders finely ground
By Divine Pestles
In the Mortars of our Skulls
To know a single serene
Antispasmodic and Diaphoretic line.

Is it I who speaks Your name
That you may know your Self:
A millipede trespassing across synapses
At the most inconvenient times—
In the rare serendipitous dream
Of Limitless Time/Space
Seizing upon Everything (almost)
Before utterance?

This is the ozone room.
You are a thin vapour
A marauding thread.
Too real to live only
In someone's head,
In the dance of trust
And careful balance
You are a hand letting go
Too fast on purpose
And a hard careen
Into the green stain
Of spring grass.

IV

I become speechless
In order to love you
Like a man, sheathe
Consciousness
In a visceral scabbard
Anaesthetize
The tongue.

The sound of one hand
Clapping
Is applause
For dissolution

And so this map of a map badly drawn:
Troubled countries and cavernous gulfs
White raging water and cataract's edge,
Sharp fissures in ancient rock, perpetual frost,
Strange naturally occurring alloys

And there are the dimensionless aeons
Into which, in each other's defense,
We have absconded
To wait out the next umpteen
Karmic glaciations:
Halley and Kohoutek
Hyakutake and Hale-Bopp
Rocky and Bullwinkle
In a rubber raft
Headed to Mooselvania.

V

To you the endless poems that might be writ
To you the blurry margins of numberless fog-strewn bays
To you these shady excrescences of wit
This hour are given
To recapitulate our days—

Mere stays of execution
Ropes scarcely knotted,
Cowl misplaced, no keys to the tower:
The covenant of the eleventh hour.

All hours are purple hours in which the daimons list
Like poorly stowed ships leery of their freight.
All prayers are purple grist
For phantom mills weary of their fate.

I have neither song enough for this
Nor courage not to sing.

I should have been content to record
The glimmer in the gloam
Of constellations behind your head
The rise of the Evening Star near your ear
The hue of your shadow falling behind you
Twilight's green shade.

I ripped you from me in these songs
And then I killed the singer.

Now there is just the incomprehensible salt
That seasons all things.

Disembodiment

And so to you my erstwhile Muse
I'll never turn again
A new giddy passion to diffuse.
Wizards are more bracing than bards,
And racier than some schmaltzy King of Hearts,
Leering from a stacked deck of cards.

You know it was your sang-froid,
Your slightly salty aplomb,
The hint of saffron in your eyes,
Your glib ad lib alchemical grin,
The psychic foie gras of your cagey nonchalance,
The flying trapeze of your intellectual poise,
The images that sauntered by in your wake,
The torch songs and swan songs,
The exponential puns.
These were not minstrel's icons or arts,
And you were not a lout strumming a lute,
No Joe Pass *manqué* with a Provençal twist.

And I don't miss
The hot rhythmic whirl of
Spiced spirits
Wearing psychedelic sarongs,
The semi-precious wavelengths
Of jokes made smoky quartz,
The fake hermetic tapestries
Of rattan and raffia and hemp
The vindaloo mind games
Hearts and bodies and souls,
Exempt.

The Arrogance of Selves

Others are essential oils Selves
Sell in sundry New Age shoppes.
Corked into tiny vials they are
Philters for all that ails
With their charged crystal eyes
And geode hearts
They are dream catchers
Mass produced.

Others are spoils Selves toil to excavate
Roping off grids in the Grail to dig and beg
The uncanny archaeology of some consummate moment—
Eternal Now, to beg the point and beg to differ
Always to differ.

The Other wears saffron and has a shaven head
The Other cultivates streetcorner stillness and is *never* perverse
Satoried fingers knotted around a small brass bowl

A short block south, Self
In gaudy tartan kilt, tam on the ground
Pipes the Highroad path from the Lowroad
And gets thirty bucks for every loonie
The Other draws.

The Other acknowledges no alms
And barely satiates hunger or thirst,
And, notwithstanding the hornpipe hustle
Gets to Scotland first.

Golf

And so we trade sweet kisses
And sentient spring skies
For chronic silence.
Vanish into exclusive lives
Guarded by truths, half-truths and lies
Where only bleak worldly things hold sway—the laws
Of banks, amortization and reasonable rates.

For a new life, press one.
For corporate abuse, press two.
For stale dates or to speak to a special agent,
Please stay on the line.
To have your head examined, press nine.

Don't worry
There are drugs
For every imaginable complaint
Ones to make you fuzzy
Anaesthetized, neutral, sedate.
Ones to take you out
Ready or not.

If nothing works
Try kundalini yoga, blue algae
And organic goatsmilk shakes
A little pop tantra
And buy a Harley.

By all means get a guru,
Get a guide—get Guido
(in 'gator Gucci)
Hire a consultant
Pay a psychic
Get your energy
Professionally analyzed
Pre-authorize
Your payments
Get a life
And some environmentally friendly
Mutual funds.

Hey babe,
I wanna sleep with
Your golf scores
For the rest of my life.

Closing Time

At last the last muse
Has shuffled out the door
And I struggle to heave a sigh
And to worm out of the sigh
One real tone, even a groan
From this zone of freedom
This season without
The subtle whining in the synapses
Of low grade brain infection.

Sure, the thunder still emanates
Up through the balls of my feet
And the hectic sky
In cyan chorus reiterates its odes.

Some sets of human eyes
Are beautiful with mortal shine
And the comet wine's
Been bottled.

I no longer see the hands beyond the hands
Lips are merely flesh
And some shapes are sublime
And some are ugly with grime
And some are torn by time
And some speak in rhymes
And some are soft with secrets
And some are crooked with crimes

And oh the hunkering bodies
The awkward limbs
The dancer's spine
The hymns to earth in the lover's hair
The freshly showered morning bodies
The cowering bones of air

The wind in hollow bones that chime
The heavy footfalls of approaching grief
The scurrying steps of fleeing years
The stealthy sabotage of heart-break
Love's gumshoe/soft-shoe,
Transcendental thief.

And from this edge
No brinkmanship
And from this brink
No dazzle
And from this harp
No old/new trill
No intoxication
No song

Gong
Spring thunder
Forbidden sleep
Green lightning

Valentine's Day 2000

Oh, what do any of us learn
In the blizzard bad trance
Of a stay-at-home day?
That Love shovels the path
For more snow to fall
To cover the tracks
Of the bearer of this bouquet:

The exhausted blooms of a life's illusions
The sick-sweet hope for an ultimate tryst
The devastated stems of carnal confusions
Wax petals that molten desire has kissed

The wireless desireless mixed messages
The perfect fake-out
The wrong guy
The wrong time
The wrong place
The wrong butt
The wrong knob
The wrong tits
The wrong vogue
Incompatible wits
The long wrong way
The bungled stake-out

A shoeless dream, a bitter cuisine, a bad scene
A neat lie, a gagged sigh, a Munchian Scream
High-octane self-igniting autodamnation
Hearts in quasi spontaneous combustion
Short-circuited would-be sentient minds
Yogic in and out breaths
Throbbing chakras, tantric calisthenics,
Mantic micro-moans
Philosopher's kidney stones

The renovated patience
The and/or gasmic grand chasms
The wrong map of the wrong neighbourhood
The wrong coincidence in the wrong hot tub
With the wrong coincidence

The right key to the wrong room
The right words on the wrong midnight
The right vibe at the wrong moment
The wannabe passions, the hots *manqué*
The bad hair day, missed signals
The wrong second guesses
The telekinetically unbent un-nested spoons
The derisive Uri Geller moons
The laughter of goon squad bedroom wraiths

Arctic sheets of unrequited heat
Allergenic high-end Mediterranean perfumes
Gut-knots, yeah-buts, skewers of rejection
Emotional laryngitis
Necrotizing pelvic neuritis
The hell freezing over of yes
Bullshit luck
Nothing sacred

Sacred nothing
Empty way
Tao of now
Divine absence

Smooth satori
Non-nirvana
Unflesh, etheric essence
Disinterested energy
Free chi
Autonomous emanation
Solar and sunless
Solo detachment
Oneness

Shadow Work

By way of neo-Nietzschean glitch
The uber-id jitterbugs
Into every mortal ditch
And summons complicit thugs

And with uncertain lunar thirst
Ink-blot-Quixote with tilt and parry and thrust
Bolts at screech of rocket launch and must
Muster the skullduggery to guess the worst.

So chalk up a list of darker hours
In dark disorderly houses with morphine laced beers
And sundry brazen shrunken heads
Whose astral laughter deftly scours
The precipitate salt in the tracks of tears
That endears other to each in rented beds.

Thus begs the coroner: stop and burst
The love-clotted geyser of noxious lust
And write upon crime's skein the first
Toxic kiss, the sting, the subatomic fuss.

So tattoo iridium asps upon the witch's dugs
Hail the nether goddess as a twisted bitch
Swallow the Shadow from rhyme frosted mugs
And scratch the preternatural itch.

Temporary Sanity

I slept through the earthquake
And have been lately reduced
To sampling the latest
In insect cuisines—
Instead of fresh greens
Before me is a platter
Of bugs in aspic
And during dinner
A conga line of itinerant drunks
Staggers and swaggers by my table
Incanting a maudlin mantra
For the one-nine-hundred lines.

The newest avatar of my single obsession
Hoodwinks me in the middle of the ordinary,
In a brasserie full of play-off hockey fans
And summons forth
All the scofflaw vampirism of my soul.

Ah, we are indiscreet, my friend,
When crossing midnight, kisses
Are concrete and dreams
Like forensic cop-artist sidewalk chalkers
Sketch out suspects, stoolies, stalkers,
Who'll frame us in a zany Spring tableau—
Ditching our chaps
At a hot erotic rodeo

He shoots! He scores!

But at the Village Brass
There is no bucking bronco
Or silky lasso

Just some sodden Habs fans
And a couple of leftover slurs
In a gaudy cartoon bubble
Sounding by themselves.

Conditional Future

We are all merely theoretical.
Perhaps we should bar code our heads
And study foreign shipping gestalts
Become professional mourners at pre-paid plots.

We could be the punch line of a tasteless joke
And a hazardous reconnaissance.
Love could cower behind a dumpster
Camouflaged by broken glass and graffiti.

We could prostrate ourselves daily
Before the Oh Well Psychopomp of What If
And perform our derelict ablutions
With semi-maybes and demi-don'ts.

We may always be
Half of a withheld
Panhandled
Kiss

Too much depends
Upon
A red
Eighteen wheeler
Full of Talmudic
Scholarship
Beside the
Yellow
Pro-No-Fault
Cop-out lobbyist
Chickens

I Should Set the Story out Step by Step

When the student is weary, the teacher nears.
When the Lover is ready, the Beloved disappears.

I should set the story out step by step
As long as a walk to the corner dep*
When the DJ in the head sets to croon
The embarrassing sentimental tune
That we won't admit we like to anyone
Not even the moon

When *esses* of shimmering heat
Snake up from sidewalk stones
And a new love's friendly fever
Simmers in the bones

And one longs for a drink
That is wet and clear and cold
And a kiss fresh as ice
And shockingly bold

I sing the lovestruck spotlight of first sight
The stunning emanation of the Unstrange Stranger in the Night
The come-together gnosis in the premonition of a blink
That puts all sub-neutrino life in synch
That glides a spectral Zambonian swan upon a rink
And slower than a slo-mo replay of a déjà-smile
Dismantles all other unrealities with style

I should croon the epileptic afterglow of the first smooch—
The almost missed lips and bumped noses
The start/stop too early too late which side chin bonk
The next time resolve for a much smoother approach
Or wail the "was anything real" blues into midnight hues
Full of stars and stars and stars without shoes
Where lurks the uncanny shapeshifter Muse
Who travels on gamma waves, UFOs, or coach
Into speak-easy dawn for some neat solar hooch.

*dep: short for *dépanneur*, a Québecois term for a corner store.

Star Chamber

On the inside and the outside
At the borders of dimensions
Beyond the tickle in the chakras
The Heart goes Bang.

Big Bang
Galaxies sing
Like coyotes in heat
Big Bang Bounty
Wanted
Alive.

Check out the rap-sheet:
Warm pistol tucked in near his dick
Two-day shadow to burn a chin
A long sunset shadow that can grin
Straight into the wild white stallion stars
And the sparks fly from their hooves
To shine up his eyes
And the screech-owl sighs in longing
For his to-die-for dead-pan.

He's a snake and a half
With a live lasso
A handsome sorry side-winder too
He polishes his platinum winged spurs
With sacred spit
Preaches true outlaw grit
And triple-dares
All thresholds.

He'll always cross his fingers in a lie
His tongue's the quickest draw against evil eye and hex
And sometimes while giving, taking and, faking sex
He shakes fists full of laughter
At the wily star-crossed sky
And sniffs for the ozone miles off

Of heat storms way out past the ridge.
He'll treat you almost good
Sometimes if you're lucky
And keep a few cold ones for him
In your fridge.

He's his own Star Chamber, never doubt it.
He writes in spirit indigo the blues he's gonna make
He writes in sacrificial blood the rules he's gonna break
He writes in vanishing ink the love notes that he'll send
Someday, maybe, if he gets a chance and doesn't forget
Your name around the next interstellar bend
Or where he left his pants.

So where, now, that rugged and ready rascal
That rake of a rodeo hound?
In some moon cave saloon
Long gone into sound
Lips all hoary with his lastest round
Tongue wagging and waltzing
Silver six-shooter tongue

He's drinking in the Venusshine
From dilated witch-hour wells
Of cosmic bedroom eyes
Wide with blue black crow-feather mascara.
He's with mountain lion mama
Purring funky frequencies
Into quasar coming skies.

Origins

Everything has fallen here from space.
The Earth is the stuff of comets
Crazy-glued together, pressurized
Into metals and rocks. Even water
Comes from between the stars
And grins its cold molecular signature
Into warp—or thaws into a gazillion
Oceanic planets.

Sundry universes are chilling out, simmering
Or about to boil, six have recently vapourized
In order to distill essence into species
And trap themselves in deoxyribonucleic worlds.

Here, under the ultra fine rain of cometary shards,
Under unnamed comets incarnate
We are vapour and clay
Making lo-fi recordings
Of starry light

In the great around again
On the blue shift strings
Of awesome lyres
We'll strum the arcane arpeggios
From each other's forsaken songbooks
And desires.

Oh, close up and from light-years off
You are alien, you are other
Separate, unknowable, unspeakable, a cipher:
A subversive nudist de-ascending an Escher staircase
A half-in-the bag Torquemada of superb inner torture
You are a seraphic Syrinx
And some kind of shrink-wrapped Panic jazz
You are sensual sapphire swing—and here's the thing
You are an imagined embrace
That bends the spine's low note
Up seven full tones
I ache to speak in tongues with you at length,
And jump your peerless bones.

Divination

When late and sleepless a poem intrudes
With ineluctable notes and effusive moods
The eyes, heavy-lidded dare not be closed
Lest a veil be lifted and a vision exposed:

The three of kisses, the five of embraces
The seven of lovers with changing faces
The dizzying thin air of the heart's cooler places
The exalted orbit where a rogue comet races

These I sing in some other life
Where I am not woman, lover,
Mother
Or any man's wife
And into the skein of space and time
I weave a hieroglyphic rhyme
To join the kismet music so sublime
To word and sign and Sacred Other.

Cernunos

To the threefold you
I owe some burnings
Some wanton messages
Some moon dark
Moon full
Spring summer fall winter
Turnings and returnings
I owe some songs
In bizarre shamanic
Open tunings

Where these abide as one
I am: a series of portals
Facets of a singular soft ruby

In this knowing,
We come-to:
Buttered mussels
Drops of real wine
Heaps of cockle-shells
Familiar scents

Raw honey
The iodine sea air
Wild sage, our sweats
Phantom vapours
As lovers knowing
How not to touch
And knowing
Nothing at all

But with moss
And peat and mead
With sorrel, salsify
And seaweed
Virgin oils
And oils of nuts
With strong spirits
Pungent smokes
Of hickories
Of alders
Of oaks

And with salt
Not touching
Not touching but knowing

With spikenard and with cloves
And with strong preserving spices
Two hearts
In one urn
Embalmed

With poppy
And with sunflower blood
Drunk butterflies
Waltzing

Without knowing
But touching and burning
Awake in violet lightning
We see

Burning	knowing	touching
Knowing	touching	burning
Touching	burning	knowing

Threefold
We

For Aesop

The finest wines are made from the grapes that grow in Comet years

The grapes were sweet
Out of reach
A green and purple stun
Of clusters
Drooping
On a sinuous vine
Each tiny globe
Artfully cruised
By a comet

Damn sweet,
Perfect for tongues and teeth
For press and squeeze
For vintage appellation
A full measure too
Of sun, rain, earth
And exotic pulsars
The moon and her minions
Tangled in nets of clear veins

They were the sweetest grapes
I've ever almost tasted
And the magic merlot
That could've stained my lips
With Dionysian delights divine
Another quaffs with quotidian SAQ* sips
Like any ordinary wine

The grapes! The grapes!
The demon-sweet
Impossible grapes.

*SAQ: *Société des alcools de Québec*, Québec provincial liquor store outlets

Love's Beams

I

We are always/never strangers in the stars
And whether far or near in galactic miles
Let's not rue the spontaneous smiles
That lit an evening's sorrows and wiles
With the real thing
Breaking and borrowing a string
And a tentative smoky entente
Among badly tuned guitars

It's terror to play the bewildering cards
That ace and deuce and trump do tend
Toward catastrophic harmonies
Of lover, soul mate and friend.
So at least, at most, as Thrice Great Allies
And best first mates we'll tack
Into brighter winds that wend
With sea-shanties o'er rip-tides
Where undertows bend
Strong rigging and ropes
And ride out the trend
Of an insane age, foolish and fearless
And barmy as bards

II

Now in limited onshore leaves
We sometimes play at mixing potions,
Trading schemes and chords
And helping slim chances
Guard the hoards
In Energy's smithy
By tempering swords
To blades of strong grass
And drinking gourds
And trill with wee hour cricket pipes
The thrills that chase Clear Light
Into dancing dawn's first ray

So wisely winks the glacial ice
In July's humid crystal.
We dream in sweats
And sweat in dreams
To know and remember
In a heartbeat's expectant systole
The heavy lightness
Of the beams

Here Stops the Mystery of Hermes and Hekate

Here stops the mystery of Hermes and Hekate
At crossroads late in ages spun
From nether archives—when all were ended and begun.
And at the beck and plea
Of the primordially scary
Threefold We
Gnash teeth and weep
Into every useless vision
Of crypto-erotic being fission
Of eroto-cryptic panic fusion
The grandest joke
Of a grander illusion
That carved bright wands
From a Hazel tree.

Would that physical stars could cross
In hat trick midnights and widdershins tunes
In the lustrous fluid of cadence point moons
Where dragons confide to the nearest cartoons
The Doonesbury sanity of a sacred gloss:
A planet grinning behind propolis clouds
At mummified mice with bee lacquer shrouds
And a blade that weighs the salmon's loss
In upstream spawning pitch and toss
Of alchemy's rapid runes.

All the dreams that zing the night
With dark giant waves that spill salt into sight
Change neap tides into reeling trances
About the jinx bamboozlement of circumstances…

Please sing the interval of a kinder creed:
Strong magic, strong medicine, strong mead.

Secret Agents

When you sip from hidden sleep
And read the dead star scrolls
When you chant the mantras of coalescence
And can synch out-of-body mutual volts
Into antigrav quintessence

When you hear the broad band
Waves and splashes
From a portable ring
Of faery stones, hell,
Then you can dig the metatones
Transmodalities
And the funny frequency maps

Between rare power naps
Skulls full of solar wind
And gulping spring planets
We've already paid the price
In monsters of the slickest sort

So if the fix is in
Or the scam's the groove
Don't move, doctor the spin
Or stoop to retort
Just deep six the vision
In your guts and genes
And be
A True Free Lover
With no liens.

Slow to Know the Chasms that Stretch Through Inner Space

Slow to know the chasms that stretch through inner space
And how the World with cash bound into its rough braids
Can tangle weak selves into selves that cringe from grace
And smooth away all Otherness with pumice and pomades,
The mortal body, but a play within a play with infinite digressions,
Sings electrical and with transient lunar sighs must ride
The side-slip rhythms of the androgynous middle tide
And stand in soup-lines with tin-cup lessons.
Heavenly bodies exhale intelligence as pervasive as light,
Inhale the history of Earth and her disturbing human scent.
Oh, who has brushed rebel comets from her hair this imminent night
And spun the dervish galaxies inward from laughter, outward from lament?
She would as soon with silver scimitar divorce me from my head
As send the cosmic Green Man with his ocarina to my bed.

Sweet, Raw Love Never Mocks

Sweet, raw Love never mocks
The vagabond who through His mysteries walks
But never takes the golden dart, the hobo who, slain
By Sophist's and Theosophist's blades
Or hog-tied by Reason's tirades and rough rope,
May only cope with Love as a mild decoction
Or balm. And so, a salve only,
Who should be our Salvation,
Love seethes Himself in a cauldron pot,
And delivers Himself, steamed, braised and poached,
Arse-up upon a starry platter.

And then, through Night's diaphanous psychic gauze,
Our shades we view as silhouettes, languid and undone
Beyond all veils, anointed and hence emitting light,
All of us simultaneously emitting ectoplasm
Into the etheric containment field...
I mean, it's enough to liquefy rock.

It is for Others that We Suspend the Rules

It is for others that we suspend the rules
Ourselves we keep in rough unwieldy yokes
Of shallow eelgrass blues that beach the heart
Of desperate perfection in a glass of ale
Of bowling ball moons and high-hat stars,
Of smooth licks and riffs and nice chops
Of frisbee metaphysics
And festive confusions

We must suspend the rules.
The ice that sleeps in deep wood's shade
Sings forth tender fern spirals.
The soaking loam grins into Passover.
The sunsets spill into suppers

Even the nearly dead
Rejoice at the changes.

The suspension of the rules
Is a complete dispensation.

To the Poets of the World

To the poets of the world
Are hard tests given
Hovering over grooves
With warped mandolins
Tone-deaf and rhythmically challenged,
Getting psyched out
And psyched in
And psyched over
Escaping the harlequinade of doubt
By pasting on new primal masks

It is exile.
The poet is a lost cause
Or tribe,
A wandering consciousness
Under the mysterious goddess moon and night.

Too slick
To commit to water only
For days on end,
We turn wine into words
And fake the miracles.

Just because it's a mystery,
Never knowing when some satyr or dryad
Will beg us for a deep electromagnetic connection
Or if, miles high in a jet
And zooming over the world
We give over to the ocean
Or pace narrow revolutionary streets.

There may be nothing
Beyond surviving
And the hard haul of the portage
Dangerous white water
Notes on birch
And the sordid inventories
And the winter wives

There may be only
The wink and shrug
Of the vampire in the hallway

And the shock of voicing
Too much
Out loud.

In the Name of Love

In the name of love
Revile love's eeriest edges

In the name of Love
Snub the wine bearer
Tip the prohibitionist
Become a born against religion

In the name of Love
Chasten Love, chastise
The smile wrapped 'round a merry secret
Invent new dangerous dualities
To hunt dynamic duos

In the name of Love
Hard-wire Hatred.

In the name of Freedom,
Enslave.

In the womb of the Mother
Sew shame.

In the mind of the Father
Plant blame.

At birth feasts
Drink original dust
And obsolescence,

In the name of Love
Keep a grip while in the grip
Of these obliterating aches.

Suspend old rules
When old rules blight,
Celebrate our partly innocent mistakes
The hands and bodies that we use
The visions that we find and lose
Our restraints
And our relaxes

In the name of Love
A toast to the Fools and Tricksters and Mimes
Who surrender strophes and rhymes
On heady lunar cliffs
And in sizzling solar canyons

In the name of Love
Carry wild honey wine
To all Love's human Companions.

I Shall Not Name You Yet

I shall not name you yet,
I shall endeavour to forget
I shall want nothing but my measly lot,
I shall smoke pot,
I will with dark self-hatred
Throw a wrench
I will with missing you declare
A game misconduct:
We are benched.

And if in a someday midnight cup of coffee, black
I withhold kisses (but blow them at your back)
Is it any wonder that I, dumbfounded, sit and stare
At Orion and the young horned moon and numbly dare
This poem to shine with Love's secret shellac?

In your inaudible whisper
I hear distant meteors laugh and sing
As galactic angels play
Cat's cradle
With electromagnetic string

The maybe of your touch,
Is a superconductor
That makes gravity come unhitched
And unmoors the dread drag
Of body unto body.
The maybe of your kiss
Is instant escape velocity
And the edge of warp
That dismantles our subatomic architectures
And reconfigures us else-here.

Your private and sovereign beauty
Has the power to enthrall
The crocus from the earth
And send the northern lights reeling
In sudden paranormal polkas
Aha! Checkmate.
All are entirely smitten.
Aha! And Aha!

Conscious Only of the Photo-Erotic Air

Conscious only of the photo-erotic air
And with a new grass swoon wound round my brain
An abject idiot I stand among the spring pines and gawk
Into the azure seizure sky and spy a soaring hawk
And guru Pan from behind some yew indecently feigns
A wink with his goat third-eye and then with a capricious glare
He hoofs it away in a mossy kilt and makes his oatpipes blare.
No far and wee balloonman mudlucious from warm rains
No oracle pestered with penny or with yarrow stalk
But a cloven mazurka and some thaw-crazy talk
My bio-psychic architecture does amply entertain
Which steams clear sap towards its sweetest dare:
To charge into a riotous gavotte he'll trick me
Into vernal buds and blooms—and then he'll lick me.

The Flesh is Willing, but the Spirit is Weak

The flesh is willing, but the spirit is weak.
I love you but I cannot speak.
I know you know, I know you know
I know you, I you, you I, I Thou.
The heart is open, but the mind is closed.
I feel you but I cannot think.
I hear you but I cannot see.
I see you but I cannot touch.
I touch you without hands.

The body is short but desire is long
I need you but I cannot move
I want you but I am not free
You I and I Thee maybe
Always never maybe
And eternally
Here but not here
And not there either.

I love you always other
Willing and unwilling
Yielding to unwilling
Yielding to yielding
But unwilling to yield
I surrender and you are gone
You vanish and I am
Deeply hidden

In sudden laughter
We are one
Flesh willing
Spirit strong
Love and Will singing
The same vital song.

Words of Absence

I go alone
I sleep alone at the bottom
Of the Well.
I see stars,
I fear stars.
There is too much shock
In the Voice of Thunder.

I go alone
I hear the Locrian
Laughter of loons
I drink mead moons
And blow kisses
To blue herons

I go alone
I stagger over bogs
I summon fogs
I erupt on your body

I go alone
I have stolen
All of your interim emotions
I have eaten
All your bridges
I have disowned you.

I go alone
To resavour
Your wormwood kiss;
Your dark, secret radio bands
And uncanny radiance

I go alone
Untouchable
Into absence.

In your Presence
I was mortified.

Titles

Beautiful Loser
Village Drunk
Acme Schmoozer
Anythingarian Monk
Gizmo-ite Neo-tsarist
Quarter-Gitano jazz Guitarist
Closet Kabbalist
Scrambler of Schemes
Hotshot Herbalist
Dealer of Dreams
Grand Magus
Of All-Purpose
Fool-Proof
Mesmerisms
Pasha of Piquant Paroxysms
Fast Talker
Smooth Seducer
Erotic as all get out
Cocksure Con, Kickass Cad,
Cynosure of Clout!

I adore thee!
I adore thee!
The mundane is reversed!
Alpha is to Omega
As Last is to First.

Our Path is Wee Hour Dark

Our path is wee hour dark
Our dawns are undrawn borders
We keep the miracles in short supply
With lip-service to dead orders
Our foolish lives contrive to keep
Our lots and lawns well weeded
And the Archons and the Molten Core
Are defunct, no longer needed.
Our accounts are crisp and laundered
Like the percale sheets upon our beds
And shooting stars no longer rain
Synergistic mystic jellies on our heads
Love's measured in box-office hits
Forgiveness in good credit-ratings
And we'll pray forever
With our Lava-lounge Hearts
For the steamiest ether-net matings.

Begin Anywhere, Begin Here

Begin anywhere, begin here,
Begin with rain drenched hair,
A cold beer, a grin,
Begin with blue
Till it's blue again,
Indigo spiral,
Sapphire gyres
And nearly violet stars
All whirling and whistling
Strange airs
And strange ethers too
So go figure
Does anything make sense?

Laughter in thunder,
The smile in a hum,
The glide in a kayak,
Amok in the moon
Barefoot R.E.M. embers
Of love's fire-walks
The green waltzes

And so I crave an out-of-body scintillating fling
That tilts at the windmills of anxious spring

But then with grown-up realistic respect
I know you somewhere out of time
And so to sleep and our dreams' stacked deck
That ends our angst in perfect rhyme.

Where I find you in your sulfurous galley
Distilling transubstantial bisques
And tricking ichor from fickle Kali—
Mon Amour! Monsieur le Cordon Bleu of Risques!

And Now Poems and Hair are Burned in Bars

And now poems and hair are burned in bars
And the talk is of nude men ascending the stairs
Of love as captured in a borrowed bed
Of marriage as Alcatraz
Of making all the wrong moves
For all the right reasons
In the wrong seasons with the latest
Honourably discharged muse

It's about losing a sustaining vision in a non-embrace,
It's about madness that stalks the early morning hours
And mooching codeine

It's about everything that ever was and wasn't
And the nothing that interfered
It's the hours of psychic traffic on the bridge of sighs
And knowing every new obsession
As an all-too-human scream

So guide this fury into deepest bedrock
Lest sharp stone axes be hurled into unsuspecting skulls
Lest concealed blades be whetted and blunt objects dulled
Lest poisons be concocted and voodoo dolls sewn.
Take this immanent violence and transform
Straight razor into smooth and hollow bone
Arsenic to almonds, agaric to alms.

With Numbness Wrapped Round Each Live Nerve

With numbness wrapped round each live nerve
With necks and other bones broken
With limbs near gangrenous and madness
Like a clock face swarmed over with flies
With freaked-out animal terrors
And a cussing id that rents the night
With the round world like some spitball
Striking with ludicrous strikeouts,
With cheap shot triple entendres etc.

If, as a way to begin, an eerie inner voice
Would moan some moldy autumn music
Or rake the nerves into loose coalitions

If, as a way to buy some time,
Winking visions waylay the messenger
And overtake sweet wild rhyme
With strong preserving spice

If love were mulled not cloven
Or sharpened with mace
And a wanton wandering bard could take
A down wind hint of far off victuals and provisions

Then would we never balk
The sacred choice to risk and risk again
Old stand-by habits for a new mistake
And taste in our first words a kiss and a fission?

Alas! Some Words've Been Lost it Seems

Alas! Some words've been lost it seems
Words with dipped cigars and espressos
Words with raised and worried eyebrows
Words that drip with sensual steam condensed
By cool sighs and fresh whispers

The words for kisses we can almost taste
That land like flying saucers on half-dreaming lips,
Utterly alien utterances under breath
Words that weep until they laugh at death
And die unspoken
Words that lie in wait and words that stalk
The autumn village leaf-strewn streets
Eight-foot tall in Day-Glo purple platform boots
And summon out from trench coat sleeves
A coven of leather goddesses
Words for you and words for me
And words yet for a zillion rent-a-visions

Words that win the guffaws of unknown muses
Words that are our covenant
Burnt into stone and hidden in an ark
Secret, sacred words
Glowing in the dark.

Notes to a Different Muse

There's a ragtime riff in every prospective muse
There's blues and then there's blues
There's hands that heal with their tunes
There's a someday in your smile
And a never in your frown
There's a silent gasp in your eyes
As raw lips grip the ice and you sashay into town
And there's the one that got away
The forever sacred grove
A fast swimming fish
In a private cove
And unrisen loaves
And basket of phrases
A miracle transmitted from above
And there's love, love, love, love
Crazy love

The Ending is the Poem I Cannot Write

The ending is the poem I cannot write
Why name tears that are wordless
Hands that cannot hold
Lips that cannot kiss
No limbs merry with seasonal dances,
No feast fires burning in stone caves
And on ancient hills.
We two once
Beneath foreign stars
Upon a stranger's roof
Were bewildered into hearing
The same eternal, wild song.

In our first young dawn
We came into knowing
Our rebirth in eachother
Before all else
And all the lights in the firmament
Chorused joyful secrets.
I know only
The garden
Of our joining
Which is the Temple Love
And Home.

The Heart's True Tones

The heart's true tones, Beloved, if there is anything written in stone
Are old in reverence for those deepest never bygone times,
En/revisioning the simple we in wavering spirit songs,
Time coming and time going, the future's mysterious kiss
Owns us in its fire by disowning, us, never owing, myriad anything.
Refinements arc into sharp salt air, young dolphins
Over seas sunmoonlit, at play, are hardly spent—
They whistle us refreshed, reclaimed in Love's wise starry firmament
And with infant's rattle, shaman's rattle and rattle of brittle bones
In shattering change, the heart's true tones
Are All and One
Here-now-there-then
In joyous unison.

The Intimate is yet Forbidden to Sing Though Spring

The intimate is yet forbidden to sing though spring
Again draws her first new flowers from the earth
Warm electrical resin is charged with sweet sweats
And the tears of inner womanly desires,
Dreams of sudden rushes of elixirs, spilling over in spite of fears
The first sweet surprise convulsions of anxious new love,
Freshness of the close proximity of unprecedented arms,
Eyes lips to close with fugitive kisses
That chatter in veins and deep hidden gorges
Like thrilled April fool's birds
Two heartbeats before dawn

And in the Body no More Anger

And in the body no more anger
Just the ache of slow thaw
And the shed of winter armour
Two pains, unfamiliar lightness
Awkward nakedness
Unsteadiness from the loss
Of burdens carried and worn too long
And the heart wishing to run
Full speed toward home
Must wait for new sap
To run through limbs
And for roots to drink
Warm rains again

I listen for goose noise
Most mornings
To retune
And return us.

A Summer Fool

I am a dream swallowed by the World
I am a world in dream's hollows
I am a fever that shatters all bones
I am death and I am sorrow
I am a photograph of a mask
I am a crossed signal
I am a spider on a spine bridge
I am a tongue of flame that speaks
I am a sculptor without hands
I am a broken neck and a shattered mind
I am a stone skipped into and out of dimensions
I am neolithic ancestral voices
I am rattles and whistles and drums
I am glistering sun in a fledgling's eye
I am the kiss of utter darkness
I am Lover, Beloved,
I am bodiless
I am an oft imagined tryst
I am a twisted road and a straight path
I am an ocean of grief
I am empty wrath
I am mythic wine
I am water and breath
I am you

Difficulty at the Beginning

Only dissolution at the greatness of heaven
Only the correct action at the correct time
Only know the way inside of the completely unknown
Dangerous rivers and dangerous crossings
Where No Self briefly stands by

The Gold Elixir and the Stone are two pursuits
That lead through treacherous wastes and subtle hells
And to the lesser agonies of limbo,
Mere suspense as all ferments toward a smooth, robust union.
Some wine is still but sunshine,
Some vintages old as Atlantean Light
And wild honey from another Earth,
Sweetened sunshine most preferred by regenerative life

Who hasn't while filled with innocence
Known upon the tongue the sugars that please,
The dripping figs, the scent of orchard blossoms
Heather and wild mountain thyme.
These are Love's intoxications and the untameable shine
In Lover's eyes as full of moon and stars
As of noon and midnight midsummers
Where garments are shed and bodies are fed
By benevolent elements

Oh, what has made a crime of desire
But some imperialism of the soul
That craves the total appropriation of essence
And even ownership of the heavens—
What should be the joy of mingling and celebration
And natural delight has become a dark banquet
Of private properties.
Our temples were made to know
In Love's heartbeats, sweats, heats,
Longings and limbs
The mysterious shivers of surrender
To the Entirely Divine

And yet so much of worldly law
Has woven itself into the blood,
Even our mental maps
Are intricate territorial screams.
The high seas of romance
Have all been charted
And the farthest stars are thwarted
With human schemes
Dreams now
Are only electro-chemical noise.
How then may two hearts open
In One Thing
And not be terrified?

So Back to the Primal Garden

So back to the primal garden
Where 'gan this weird ferment
Wild honey from rock
Transformed to heady mead
A dance through the labyrinth
With golden thread
A tour of the abodes of the living,
Half-living and the dead
A rebuilt hallucination of ways
Toward the One Still Centre of All—None can pass
But the wholly surrendered and annihilated,
Terrible angels Guard the gates.

Expect every imaginable monstrosity
Threatening the complete erasure
Of your secret name—
Even ones sincerely Chinese
That don't respond to Assyro-Babylonian rites
Ah, these have ravenous turquoise tigers
Up their slick silk sleeves
That speak a sort of mandarin Greek
And drink chilled spinal fluid, neat.

Separated Minds Build Moral Fortresses and Trenches

Separated minds build moral fortresses and trenches
The body's subtle fires are suffocated
The psyche's clear fountains are evaporated.
We know one another in the One Mind,
See with the same eyes,
Hear our harmonies in our arteries
Dread our entanglement
And try to be so gentle
That nothing means.

Endless I/Thou, we elsewhere must,
Equal under heaven,
Endure the alien shudder of our love
As midnight earthquake lights in spring skies.

The myriad things and torrid imaginings
That claim Love's sacred ancestry—
The law and all its loopholes
Written in the genome,
Unnamed twins, repressed left-hand,
The tiny cyst of another's heart cells
In the limbic lobe,
The mystic call of chromosome to chromosome,
Leap of spectrums from dilated pupil to dilated pupil,
The flight, fright, fight adrenal arousals,
Flood of primal blood-song in the coiled snake,
All colour paroxysmal in the mental scape,
Forehead's door smashed wide open,
The obliteration of personal identity,
The unanimous signature of All upon All,
The darkness in all of the masters
Eavesdropping on someone's prayers,
The burgled private chambers,
The bit of goat given to the dog
The seared synapses and kiln baked cranial bones...

And then mornings, wet with the sweat of dream
Entanglements, do we rise to the scorch of sun smelling like
Eachother's salts and musks who know only the touch of astral
Hands and kiss of spirit lips?

There is a place just beneath your eye still slick
With an iridescent secret kiss
And the summer birds summon us
To the bridge of Dawn.
No wonder then the Angel is summoned
To gently untangle us, mere fools subsumed
In the awe of instant recognition
That the Lover is the Perfect Stranger
Who both shocks and attunes us to infinite surprise.

Envoi

Whatever comes must beg its art
A little from miracles, a little from dust
And find its alms in rhyming palms
And trust to spring storms and spring calms
To settle the debts of the heart

Whatever lingers
Must whistle its mirth
In limping dirges and comic lust
And know the intervals of carnivals
And hail giant night's quick animals
That compose the moon's rebirth

Whatever stays
Must keep its pack
Ready at star-rise, ready at dawn
To turn on a dime the joke of time
Invent no punishment, commit no crime
Spring ahead, and fall back.

And what goes around
Must come
To give its art in trust
To bow the head before the bed
And pray true lovers
May ever be fed
The manna of asylum.

On the Marriage of Heaven and Earth

The eyes that sometimes look out from my eyes
And mouth that curls an almost-alien smile into my lips
The inner body forces that drive an eerie duality
A half-familiar reflex in the mind, a fear that is not mine
Harmonic voice that makes one voice in two hearts singing
Where we are one, Thee and I—but on the other side
Where the World bides its time as far apart as lifetimes
Separation and connection, sorrow and joy, more sorrow than joy
Fear and love, more fear than love, dead silence and song
More silent than a Song of Songs the eternal dark light blind sight.

Ah, but your hands, your separate hands and sovereign eyes
The midnight kiss at noon of sun on both the planet's sides
The pell-mell plunge into inner/outer one space, bedrock
And the arkless deluges of longing, the cosmic inundations
The telepathic wedding in a circle of blossoming peonies
The honey stolen from the cave of the sun in a dream
The mescaline clouds and the mescaline mountains
And the breakfast of half a kiss.